101 Academic Word
An 8-year-old Must Know
(3rd Grade)

Write them & Understand them & Use them

Mastering the Vocabulary
That Advances Children's IQ Greatly

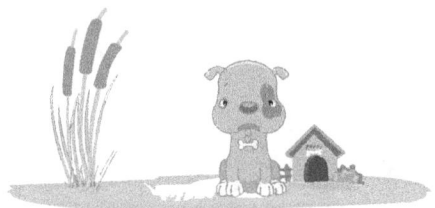

ISBN: 979-8-55-505851-5   Copyright © 2020 Derek Schuger

All rights reserved. No part of this publication may be reproduced, distributed, or transmitted in any form or by any means, including photocopying, recording, or other electronic or mechanical methods, without the prior written permission of the publisher, except in the case of brief quotations embodied in critical reviews and certain other noncommercial uses permitted by copyright law.

Intruduction

This book enlists a group of 101 academic words essential to the intellectual advancement of 8-year-old children or 3rd graders. These words are not necessarily commonly used in a day to day conversation. But they are frequently used in academic dialogue and text, classrooms and textbooks, across all subjects, such as history, math, language arts, science, or project discussions. Mastering these essential words improves study efficiency through better communication and precise presentation abilities, enhancing children's confidence toward a leadership position.

This book is a workbook that takes the traditional approach to gain vocabulary study efficiency. The learning path is easy and straightforward, the same as how we learned our vocabulary before the computer and tablet days. For each word, students write it repeatedly multiple times as instructed, then write the word's meaning and a sentence containing the word. It's a process utilizing both visual cues and hand fine-motor to stimulate brain memory, like engraving the word spelling, its meaning, and its uses into their brain memory, and retrieving it as a verbal tool as whenever they are needed. Besides, the book's practices will guarantee students' neat and beautiful handwriting.

Here are the enlisted academic words in this book.

101 Academic Word an 8-Year-Old Must Know

ability	a-bil-i-ty	the state of being able to do something.	No one knows my ability to fly like a bird because I have always flown in my imagination.
accuse	ac-cuse	to claim that someone has done something wrong.	Don't accuse me of being sneaky, I'm simply more clever than you are.
additional	ad-di-tion-al	more than what is already present.	We'll need additional help! Can anybody help? please!
agreeable	a-gree-a-ble	willing to agree.	Why do I love my dog? Because Goofery is such an agreeable companion whenever I need.
ambition	am-bi-tion	a strong desire to achieve.	My ambition is to visit all Disney parks around the world.
argue	ar-gue	to contend or disagree verbally.	Do not argue with an idiot. You'll never win.
arrange	ar-range	to organize an activity; to put things in order.	My parents are responsible for arranging the vacation trip to the waterpark. My work is to enjoy it.
assist	as-sist	help or give aid.	Hi, how may I assist you today?
attract	at-tract	to draw interest; to exert a force.	I know Jackie likes my brother Reese. She always does something to attract Reese's attention.
brilliant	bril-liant	very bright; very smart.	You're brilliant and beautiful.
careless	care-less	giving little attention; not concerned.	"Don't be so careless. It should be 'My mom is kind.' not 'My mom is kid.' You miss the letter n."
cause	cause	make something happen; a reason for something to happen.	From now on, let no one cause me trouble.
certain	cer-tain	for sure; a specific kind of.	I feel certain my daddy loves me enough to build me a treehouse in our backyard.
climate	cli-mate	condition of the weather; prevalent public opinion.	Bananas grow better in a warm and moist climate.
compare	com-pare	to find out differences or alike.	Don't compare my mind to yours. Mine is way smarter.
construct	con-struct	to build, make, or form.	Let's construct a spaceship with your LEGO.
continent	con-ti-nent	the seven continents: Africa, Antarctica, Asia, Australia, Europe, North America and South America.	Antarctica is the southernmost continent and it's the site of South Pole.
contrast	con-trast	distinct differences; to make distinct differences.	"Wow! Such is the contrast between smart and stupid."
credit	cred-it	the state or quality of being believed.	It's just not fair that Santa gets all the credit of giving out Christmas gifts, but never delivers.
culture	cul-ture	traits, such as customs, arts, and governing, of a social group.	Culture is what we eat, how we dress, the way we live, and the things we believe.
dangle	dan-gle	to hang loosely.	Don't dangle the toy in front of your kitty or it will go crazy!
deed	deed	intentionally performed action.	Assisting others is truly a good deed.
defend	de-fend	to hold out against attacks; to keep off harm and danger.	I told my parents I would defend my right to have a better gift for this Christmas. I meant I really want a real puppy.
describe	de-scribe	account of fact, condition, or event in words.	Can you describe what happened?
detail	de-tail	a particular fact or feature about something.	Please tell me what happened in detail.
develop	de-vel-op	to grow and become more advanced.	This book is designed to develop your learning skills.
disappointed	dis-ap-point-ed	sad feeling caused by unfulfilled expectation.	"You didn't finish your homework. Really? Again? I'm disappointed in you."
division	di-vi-sion	separation; an act of separating a whole into parts.	A sense of division between boys and girls in the class was growing.
effect	ef-fect	a change caused by an action.	The football hit Tommy and he was stunned. You could see a surprising effect on his face.
elect	e-lect	to select by voting.	Let's vote to elect a cheerleader.
endangered	en-dan-ger-ed	in a state of unsafe; at risk of dying out.	Pandas are one of the endangered species.

event	e-vent	a thing that occurs.	The coming 4th of July Parade will be a very fun event.
examine	ex-am-ine	to inspect or test the condition of.	Cathy leaned down to examine a tiny bug on the grass.
example	ex-am-ple	a typical thing of a group that to be imitated or not to be imitated.	Be a good example, would you?
experience	ex-pe-ri-ence	knowledge and skill from doing and seeing.	It was such an amazing experience watching Avatar in a 3D theater. Do you know what 3D is?
explore	ex-plore	travel to discover; study to find.	I'd love to explore the woods. There may be mysterious treasures hidden in there.
fatal	fa-tal	causing death.	War is a fatal event. People get killed, children lose their parents, and everything will be destroyed.
fierce	fierce	showing intense, violent, and forceful.	Where the line between good and bad of playing video games lies is a matter of fierce dispute.
flexible	flex-i-ble	able to bend or change easily without breaking.	Can we be more flexible about dinner time? I have too much homework to do today.
flutter	flut-ter	a quick and irregular movement.	Jackie waited for a long time. Seeing mom's car finally appeared in front of the entrance, she felt her heart started to flutter.
fortunate	for-tu-nate	receiving or bringing an unexpected good thing.	I was very fortunate to grow up in a time when my parents were still in love with each other. Most of my classmates didn't meet their real father or mother often.
frail	frail	unhealthy, weak, or easily broken.	Wearing a big coat, I gave them an impression of me as being frail and petite. But I was quite beefy and strong. I was a gymnast in school and I had lots of muscles.
furious	fu-ri-ous	very angry, violent, and forceful.	Mrs. Balloons would have been furious if we hadn't cleaned up that mess quickly.
gathered	gath-er-ed	coming or bringing together from different places.	My friends gathered at my house. We sat around, talked, ate, and laughed. It was fun.
gist	gist	the main point of information.	Please try to think of a short phrase that sums up the gist of the story.
globe	globe	rounded object; the world.	Humans are amazing creatures. We produce 4 babies on this globe every second, 360,000 a day. Poor earth!
gradual	grad-u-al	developing slowly in small steps.	Everything in the world is conducted by a gradual process. This seems to be the great principle of harmony in the universe.
individual	individual	a single person or thing.	If every individual has the right amount of food and exercise, not too little and not too much, that's the safest way to health.
infer	in-fer	to draw a conclusion from facts.	I don't mind my friends, teachers, mom, and daddy to infer that I have all kinds of clever ideas in my not-so-little brain.
intelligent	in-tel-li-gent	having the ability to learn and understand.	To be intelligent, one will need to be flexible and go with the flow, not to be stubborn and self-centered.
invitation	in-vi-ta-tion	the act of inviting someone to do something.	Making a good smile is an expression of warm invitation; it is an invitation to the happiness in our common humanity.
irritate	ir-ri-tate	to make someone annoyed.	Bobby scratched his head, irritated at himself for getting so caught up in the fact that Fred didn't want to play with him.
journey	jour-ney	an act of traveling; travel.	"We know it's a long journey from Canada to Disney World at Florida. But be ready, we're coming!"
limit	lim-it	the amount, level, or number beyond the point that may pass.	There's no limit to how smart a child can get, on account of one creative saying always leading to another.
magnificent	mag-nif-i-cent	very good, great, or admirable.	"You're one of the most magnificent and delightful presents God has given us."

Word	Syllables	Definition	Example
mend	mend	to fix something that is broken.	I have to mend my relation with Amy quickly because she will bring cupcakes for her birthday tomorrow. I really like cupcakes.
multiply	mul-ti-ply	to increase itself for a number of times.	To make the "multiply" really meaningful, I hope my chocolate candy bars can multiply ten times, like 2x10=20.
mystify	mys-ti-fy	to purposely make something unintelligible.	I don't know why my brain is so smart. I am always surprised and mystified by it.
nation	na-tion	a country with its own government.	I pledge allegiance to my Flag and the Republic for which it stands, one nation, indivisible, with liberty and justice for all.
nervous	nerv-ous	anxious and worried.	I always got nervous speaking in front of the class. The first sentence, I was nervous. Then after that, forget it; I'd start talking.
observe	ob-serve	to notice or to watch carefully.	I listen and talk; I also watch and observe. That's communication.
occur	oc-cur	to happen or take place.	That was an accident that occured right after lunch. I crashed into Miss Honey and knocked her down to the floor.
opponent	op-po-nent	a person who competes against another.	It's not about knocking my opponent out. It's about I don't fail.
opposite	op-po-site	a position on the other side of something; totally different.	Cathy made a face as she sat in the chair opposite her mom, "Okay, let's talk."
ordeal	or-deal	a long lasting unpleasant experience.	We're grateful for the fifteen minutes recess after a boring History class. But we also realize the ordeal that lies before us, a long Math class.
origin	or-i-gin	the beginning; the cause.	The DNA test can trace my ancestral origin back 1,000 years. I hope my ancestor was not a monkey, you know, 1,000 years!
outcome	out-come	result or effect.	If aliens visit us, I hope the outcome won't be like when Columbus landed in America. Bad idea for the native earth mankind.
passage	pas-sage	a gate or way that connects places.	I squeezed through a narrow passage on the wall and stepped into an aisle leading to an exit. I escaped safely though a little out of breath.
patient	pa-tient	able to tolerate annoyed things; one who receives medical care.	We all need to be patient and give each other a little space.
peer	peer	to look carefully; someone who has the same social position.	The microscope allows us to peer deeper into the mysteries of cells in your body.
persuade	per-suade	to make someone believe something.	How did you persuade daddy to agree to buy you a new robotic servant?
pleasant	pleas-ant	a sense of happiness and enjoyment.	There are more pleasant things to do than argue with an idiot.
predict	pre-dict	to say something that will happen in the future.	Everything changes with time. You can't predict it all. You can't even predict what's in your dream tonight.
prevent	pre-vent	to keep something from existing or occurring.	This vaccine will prevent us from getting sick.
primary	pri-ma-ry	original; the most important part.	The primary goal of space science is to discover what's unknown about the space. Actually, any science is about to discover things unknown.
purpose	pur-pose	the reason to do something; the reason something exists.	What is the purpose of you saying that? Just try to make me feel bad?
recognize	rec-og-nize	to acknowledge someone or something you knew.	I couldn't recognize myself in the mirror at first with the new makeup. It's so cool.
repair	re-pair	to fix something that is broken.	The greatness of America lies not in being more enlightened than any other nation, but rather in her ability to repair her faults.
respect	re-spect	an admiring feeling for someone or something.	With all due respect, Miss Honey, I don't think you're right in this case.

Word	Syllables	Definition	Example
responsible	re-spon-si-ble	obligated to; having control over or duty to care.	My mom is responsible for cooking Christmas dinner and my dad is in charge of decorating our house.
ridiculous	ri-dic-u-lous	unreasonable, silly, and stupid.	I have never made but one prayer to God, a very short one: 'O Lord make my enemies ridiculous.' And God granted it.
scatter	scat-ter	to move randomly far apart.	The zebras quickly scattered as the lion charged at the herd.
sensitive	sen-si-tive	highly responsive to minor changes.	This metal detector is so cool. It's sensitive enough to detect coins buried 2 feet underground.
shiver	shiv-er	shaking slightly because of cold or frightened.	"It's so cold," she said with a shiver.
signal	sig-nal	a gesture, action, or sound that conveys message.	The phone signal was not strong enough for me to make a phone call to my friends.
similar	sim-i-lar	alike but not exactly the same.	Your phone is similar to mine in shape and color.
slumber	slum-ber	in the state of sleep; to sleep.	What's a slumber party? It's a sleepover. That's it.
solution	so-lu-tion	an answer to a problem or difficult situation.	I have a solution that might save the world. Let's all move to Mars.
starve	starve	hungry; to feel severe hunger.	I grew up wanting to be an artist, but my parents were sure I would starve to death. So, they put me in a kitchen to become a chef.
struggled	strug-gled	feeling great difficult and resistant.	I struggled to be good at math, to be good at writing, to be good at whatever... But what I did not struggle with is the best of what I do, like telling stories.
stumble	stum-ble	to fall or lose balance while walking or running.	Alex was running in the woods. He stumbled on a log, fell into the thick bushes, and hurt his butt.
tackle	tack-le	to deal with a problem or difficult situation.	A bowl of ice cream always calms me down and makes my thoughts straight. Then I can tackle the problem with a fresh mind. But it does get me fat though.
triumph	tri-umph	a big victory, success, or achievement, or the feeling of it.	One of the greatest triumphs of human history is the eradication of smallpox by vaccination.
typical	typ-i-cal	the essential facts or qualities of a group of things or people.	This has been a typical day for me, having breakfast, going to school, coming back home, having dinner, doing homework, and going to bed. No time to play.
unite	u-nite	to come together for a common goal.	What's the capital of the United States? Washington, D.C.
unusual	un-u-su-al	different from commonly known.	Humans are a very, very unusual species. We dive deep in the sea, fly high in the sky, and send instant messages around the globe.
valuable	val-u-a-ble	very useful, or worth a lot of money.	what's the most valuable thing for now? The cupcake in my hands.
vast	vast	extremely great in amount, size, or intensity.	The vast majority of students in my class agreed that we should celebrate Miss Honey's birthday.
vision	vi-sion	the state of seeing; the mental images of something.	America was established to realize a vision, to realize an ideal - to discover and maintain liberty among men.
volunteer	vol-un-teer	a person who undertakes a task willingly and not getting paid.	"Why do volunteers work for free?" "Because they earn credits that worth more than money."
wander	wan-der	to walk leisurely.	"Honey, don't wander far from the house. There are strangers on the street." "Are there any good strangers?" "Yes. But we're concerning the bad ones."

To help learn the 101 academic words effectively, we have developed a new font in two formats, solid line and dotted line. What makes this font different from others is its unique rounded formation, which lies between print and cursive styles. An eight-year-old child, who has gained some fine motor skills, will master this font in no time. The dotted font allows them to trace the 101 academic words, definitions, and associated sentences. By completing this book, they will know how to use these 101 words and write beautifully too.

ABCDEFGHIJKLM
NOPQRSTUVWXY
Zabcdefghijklmnopq
rstuvwxyz ' " " ! " # $ ¢
( ) . , 0 1 2 3 4 5 6 7 8 9 : ; ?

See if you're able to trace the following glyphs.

ABCDEFGHIJKLM
NOPQRSTUVWXY
Zabcdefghijklmnopq
rstuvwxyz ' " " ! " # $ ¢ '
( ) . , 0 1 2 3 4 5 6 7 8 9 : ; ?

ability | a-bil-i-ty | the state of being able to do something.

No one knows my ability to fly like a bird because I have always flown in my imagination.

Trace the dotted words:

ability   ability   ability   ability   ability   ability

What does it mean? Trace the dotted words:

the state of being able to do something.
the state of being able to do something.

Use the word in a sentence. Trace the dotted words:

No one knows my ability to fly like a bird because I have always flown in my imagination.
No one knows my ability to fly like a bird because I have always flown in my imagination.

Handwriting Essential, trace the dotted letters:

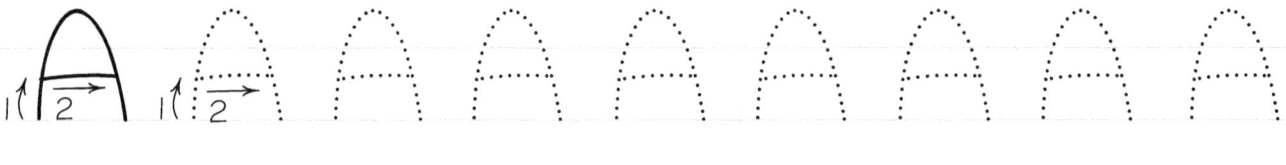

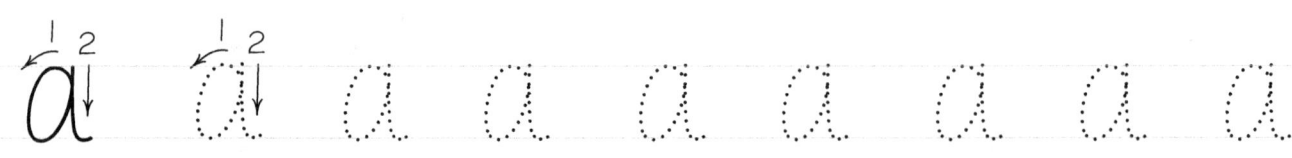

accuse | ac-cuse | to claim that someone has done something wrong.

Don't **accuse** me of being sneaky, I'm simply more clever than you are.

Trace the dotted words:

accuse   accuse   accuse   accuse   accuse

What does it mean? Trace the dotted words:

to claim that someone has done something wrong.
to claim that someone has done something wrong.

Use the word in a sentence. Trace the dotted words:

Don't accuse me of being sneaky, I'm simply more clever than you are.
Don't accuse me of being sneaky, I'm simply more clever than you are.

Handwriting Essential, trace the dotted letters:

B B B B B B B B

b b b b b b b b

additional | ad-di-tion-al | more than what is already present.

We'll need **additional** help! Can anybody help? please!

Trace the dotted words:

additional additional additional additional

What does it mean? Trace the dotted words:

more than what is already present.
more than what is already present.

Use the word in a sentence. Trace the dotted words:

We'll need additional help! Can anybody help? please!
We'll need additional help! Can anybody help? please!

Handwriting Essential, trace the dotted letters:

C C C C C C C

C C C C C C C

agreeable | a-gree-a-ble | willing to agree.

Why do I love my dog? Because Goofery is such an **agreeable** compinion whenever I need.

Trace the dotted words:

agreeable   agreeable   agreeable   agreeable

What does it mean? Trace the dotted words:

willing to agree.
willing to agree.

Use the word in a sentence. Trace the dotted words:

Why do I love my dog? Because Goofery is such an agreeable compinion whenever I need.
Why do I love my dog? Because Goofery is such an agreeable compinion whenever I need.

Handwriting Essential, trace the dotted letters:

D D D D D D D

d d d d d d d

ambition | am-bi-tion | a strong desire to achieve.

My **ambition** is to visit all Disney parks around the world.

Trace the dotted words:

ambition   ambition   ambition   ambition   ambition

What does it mean? Trace the dotted words:

a strong desire to achieve.
a strong desire to achieve.

Use the word in a sentence. Trace the dotted words:

My ambition is to visit all Disney parks around the world.
My ambition is to visit all Disney parks around the world.

Handwriting Essential, trace the dotted letters:

E E E E E E E

e e e e e e e

argue | ar-gue | to contend or disagree verbally.

Do not **argue** with an idiot. You'll never win.

Trace the dotted words:

argue   argue   argue   argue   argue   argue

What does it mean? Trace the dotted words:

to contend or disagree verbally.
to contend or disagree verbally.

Use the word in a sentence. Trace the dotted words:

Do not argue with an idiot. You'll never win.
Do not argue with an idiot. You'll never win.

Handwriting Essential, trace the dotted letters:

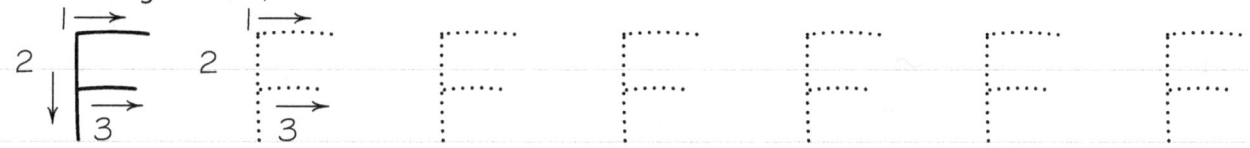

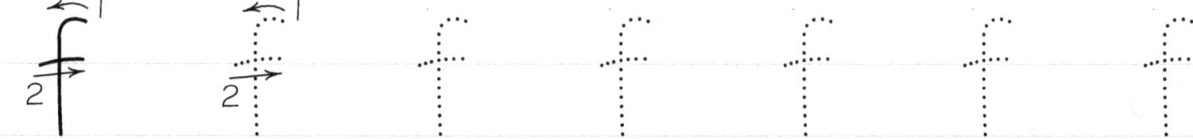

arrange | ar-range | to organize an activity; to put things in order.

My parents are responsible for **arranging** the vacation trip to the waterpark. My work is to enjoy it.

Trace the dotted words:

arrange   arrange   arrange   arrange   arrange

What does it mean? Trace the dotted words:

to organize an activity; to put things in order.
to organize an activity; to put things in order.

Use the word in a sentence. Trace the dotted words:

My parents are responsible for arranging the vacation trip to the waterpark. My work is to enjoy it.
My parents are responsible for arranging the vacation trip to the waterpark. My work is to enjoy it.

Handwriting Essential, trace the dotted letters:

G   G   G   G   G   G   G

g   g   g   g   g   g   g

assist | as-sist | help or give aid.

Hi, how may I **assist** you today?

Trace the dotted words:

assist assist assist assist assist assist

What does it mean? Trace the dotted words:

help or give aid.
help or give aid.

Use the word in a sentence. Trace the dotted words:

Hi, how may I assist you today?
Hi, how may I assist you today?

Handwriting Essential, trace the dotted letters:

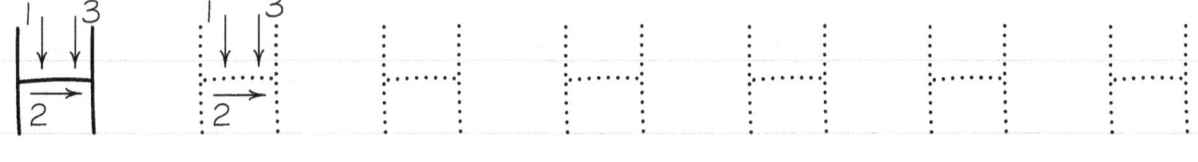

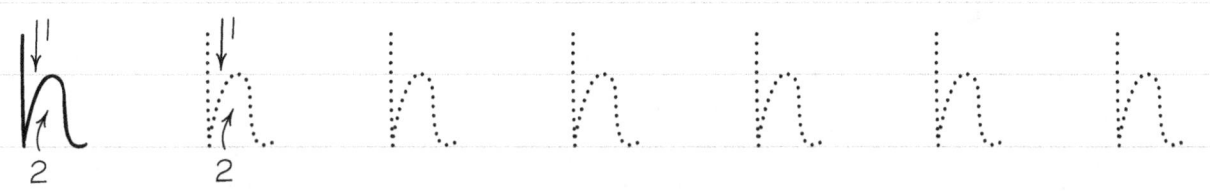

15

attract | at-tract | to draw interest; to exert a force.

I know Jackie likes my brother Reese. She always does something to **attract** Reese's attention.

Trace the dotted words:

attract   attract   attract   attract   attract

What does it mean? Trace the dotted words:

to draw interest; to exert a force.
to draw interest; to exert a force.

Use the word in a sentence. Trace the dotted words:

I know Jackie likes my brother Reese. She always does something to attract Reese's attention.
I know Jackie likes my brother Reese. She always does something to attract Reese's attention.

Handwriting Essential, trace the dotted letters:

brilliant | bril-liant | very bright; very smart.

You're **brilliant** and beautiful.

Trace the dotted words:

brilliant   brilliant   brilliant   brilliant   brilliant

What does it mean? Trace the dotted words:

very bright; very smart.
very bright; very smart.

Use the word in a sentence. Trace the dotted words:

You're brilliant and beautiful.
You're brilliant and beautiful.

Handwriting Essential, trace the dotted letters:

J   J   J   J   J   J

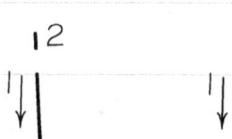   j   j   j   j   j

careless | care-less | giving little attention; not concerned.

"Don't be so **careless**. It should be 'My mom is kind.' not 'My mom is kid.' You miss the letter n."

Trace the dotted words:

careless   careless   careless   careless   careless

What does it mean? Trace the dotted words:

giving little attention; not concerned.
giving little attention; not concerned.

Use the word in a sentence. Trace the dotted words:

"Don't be so careless. It should be 'My mom is kind.' not 'My mom is kid.' You miss the letter n."
"Don't be so careless. It should be 'My mom is kind.' not 'My mom is kid.' You miss the letter n."

Handwriting Essential, trace the dotted letters:

K   K   K   K   K   K   K

k   k   k   k   k   k   k

cause | cause | make something happen; a reason for something to happen.

From now on, let no one **cause** me trouble.

Trace the dotted words:

cause   cause   cause   cause   cause   cause

What does it mean? Trace the dotted words:

make something happen; a reason for something to happen.
make something happen; a reason for something to happen.

Use the word in a sentence. Trace the dotted words:

From now on, let no one cause me trouble.
From now on, let no one cause me trouble.

Handwriting Essential, trace the dotted letters:

L   L   L   L   L   L

l   l   l   l   l   l

certain | cer-tain | for sure; a specific kind of.

I feel **certain** my daddy loves me enough to build me a treehouse in our backyard.

Trace the dotted words:

certain   certain   certain   certain   certain

What does it mean? Trace the dotted words:

for sure; a specific kind of.
for sure; a specific kind of.

Use the word in a sentence. Trace the dotted words:

I feel certain my daddy loves me enough to build me a treehouse in our backyard.
I feel certain my daddy loves me enough to build me a treehouse in our backyard.

Handwriting Essential, trace the dotted letters:

M   M   M   M   M   M

m   m   m   m   m   m

climate | cli-mate | condition of the weather; prevalent public opinion.

Bananas grow better in a warm and moist **climate**.

Trace the dotted words:

climate   climate   climate   climate   climate

What does it mean? Trace the dotted words:

condition of the weather; prevalent public opinion.

condition of the weather; prevalent public opinion.

Use the word in a sentence. Trace the dotted words:

Bananas grow better in a warm and moist climate.

Bananas grow better in a warm and moist climate.

Handwriting Essential, trace the dotted letters:

N   N   N   N   N   N   N

n   n   n   n   n   n   n

compare | com-pare | to find out differences or alike.

Don't **compare** my mind to yours. Mine is way smarter.

Trace the dotted words:

compare   compare   compare   compare   compare

What does it mean? Trace the dotted words:

to find out differences or alike.
to find out differences or alike.

Use the word in a sentence. Trace the dotted words:

Don't compare my mind to yours. Mine is way smarter.
Don't compare my mind to yours. Mine is way smarter.

Handwriting Essential, trace the dotted letters:

O O O O O O O

o o o o o o o

construct | con-struct | to build, make, or form.

Let's **construct** a spaceship with your LEGO.

Trace the dotted words:

construct   construct   construct   construct

What does it mean? Trace the dotted words:

to build, make, or form.
to build, make, or form.

Use the word in a sentence. Trace the dotted words:

Let's construct a spaceship with your LEGO.
Let's construct a spaceship with your LEGO.

Handwriting Essential, trace the dotted letters:

P P P P P P P

p p p p p p p

continent | con-ti-nent | the seven continents: Africa, Antarctica, Asia, Australia, Europe, North America, and South America.

Antarctica is the southernmost **continent** and it's the site of South Pole.

Trace the dotted words:

continent   continent   continent   continent

What does it mean? Trace the dotted words:

the seven continents: Africa, Antarctica, Asia, Australia, Europe, North America, and South America.

the seven continents: Africa, Antarctica, Asia, Australia, Europe, North America, and South America.

Use the word in a sentence. Trace the dotted words:

Antarctica is the southernmost continent and it's the site of South Pole.

Antarctica is the southernmost continent and it's the site of South Pole.

contrast | con-trast | distinct differences; to make distinct differences.

"Wow! Such is the **contrast** between smart and stupid."

Trace the dotted words:

contrast   contrast   contrast   contrast

What does it mean? Trace the dotted words:

distinct differences; to make distinct differences.
distinct differences; to make distinct differences.

Use the word in a sentence. Trace the dotted words:

"Wow! Such is the contrast between smart and stupid."
"Wow! Such is the contrast between smart and stupid."

Handwriting Essential, trace the dotted letters:

Q Q Q Q Q Q Q

q q q q q q q

credit | cred-it | the state and quality of being believed.

It's just not fair that Santa gets all the **credit** of giving out Christmas gifts, but never delivers.

Trace the dotted words:

credit credit credit credit credit credit

What does it mean? Trace the dotted words:

the state and quality of being believed.
the state and quality of being believed.

Use the word in a sentence. Trace the dotted words:

It's just not fair that Santa gets all the credit of giving out Christmas gifts, but never delivers.
It's just not fair that Santa gets all the credit of giving out Christmas gifts, but never delivers.

Handwriting Essential, trace the dotted letters:

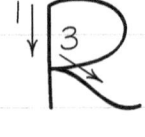 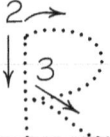 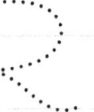 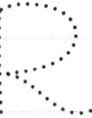 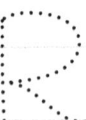 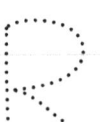 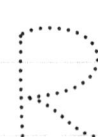

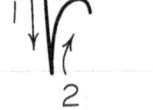 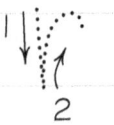 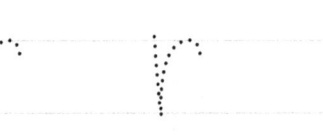 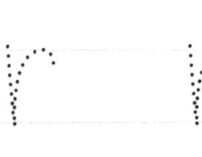 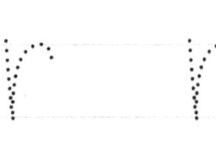

culture | cul-ture | traits, such as customs, arts, and governing, of a social group.

Culture is what we eat, how we dress, the way we live, and the things we believe.

Trace the dotted words:

culture   culture   culture   culture   culture

What does it mean? Trace the dotted words:

traits, such as customs, arts, and governing, of a social group.
traits, such as customs, arts, and governing, of a social group.

Use the word in a sentence. Trace the dotted words:

Culture is what we eat, how we dress, the way we live, and the things we believe.
Culture is what we eat, how we dress, the way we live, and the things we believe.

Handwriting Essential, trace the dotted letters:

S S S S S S S

s s s s s s s

dangle | dan-gle | to hang loosely.

Don't **dangle** the toy in front of your kitty or it will go crazy!

Trace the dotted words:

dangle   dangle   dangle   dangle   dangle   dangle

What does it mean? Trace the dotted words:

to hang loosely.
to hang loosely.

Use the word in a sentence. Trace the dotted words:

Don't dangle the toy in front of your kitty or it will go crazy!
Don't dangle the toy in front of your kitty or it will go crazy!

Handwriting Essential, trace the dotted letters:

T T T T T T T

t t t t t t t

deed | deed | intentionally performed action.

Assisting others is truly a good **deed**.

Trace the dotted words:

deed   deed   deed   deed   deed   deed   deed

What does it mean? Trace the dotted words:

intentionally performed action.
intentionally performed action.

Use the word in a sentence. Trace the dotted words:

Assisting others is truly a good deed.
Assisting others is truly a good deed.

Handwriting Essential, trace the dotted letters:

U U U U U U U

u u u u u u u

defend | de-fend | to hold out against attacks; to keep off harm and danger.

I told my parents I would **defend** my right to have a better gift for this Christmas. I meant I need a real puppy.

Trace the dotted words:

defend   defend   defend   defend   defend   defend

What does it mean? Trace the dotted words:

to hold out against attacks; to keep off harm and danger.
to hold out against attacks; to keep off harm and danger.

Use the word in a sentence. Trace the dotted words:

I told my parents I would defend my right to have a better gift for this Christmas. I meant I really want a real puppy.
I told my parents I would defend my right to have a better gift for this Christmas. I meant I really want a real puppy.

describe | de-scribe | account of fact, condition, or event in words.

Can you **describe** what happened?

Trace the dotted words:

describe   describe   describe   describe

What does it mean? Trace the dotted words:

account of fact, condition, or event in words.
account of fact, condition, or event in words.

Use the word in a sentence. Trace the dotted words:

Can you describe what happened?
Can you describe what happened?

Handwriting Essential, trace the dotted letters:

V V V V V V V

v v v v v v v

detail | de-tail | a particular fact or feature about something.

Please tell me what happened in **detail**.

Trace the dotted words:

detail detail detail detail detail detail

What does it mean? Trace the dotted words:

a particular fact or feature about something.
a particular fact or feature about something.

Use the word in a sentence. Trace the dotted words:

Please tell me what happened in detail.
Please tell me what happened in detail.

Handwriting Essential, trace the dotted letters:

W W W W W W

w w w w w w

32

develop | de-vel-op | to grow and become more advanced.

This book is designed to **develop** your learning skills.

Trace the dotted words:

develop   develop   develop   develop   develop

What does it mean? Trace the dotted words:

to grow and become more advanced.
to grow and become more advanced.

Use the word in a sentence. Trace the dotted words:

This book is designed to develop your learning skills.
This book is designed to develop your learning skills.

Handwriting Essential, trace the dotted letters:

X   X   X   X   X   X

y   y   y   y   y   y

disappointed | dis-ap-point-ed | sad feeling caused by unfulfilled expectation.

"You didn't finish your homework. Really? Again? I'm **disappointed** in you."

Trace the dotted words:

disappointed   disappointed   disappointed

What does it mean? Trace the dotted words:

sad feeling caused by unfulfilled expectation.
sad feeling caused by unfulfilled expectation.

Use the word in a sentence. Trace the dotted words:

"You didn't finish your homework. Really? Again? I'm disappointed in you."
"You didn't finish your homework. Really? Again? I'm disappointed in you."

Handwriting Essential, trace the dotted letters:

Y Y Y Y Y Y Y

y y y y y y y

division | di-vi-sion | separation; an act of separating a whole into parts.

A sense of **division** between boys and girls in the class was growing.

Trace the dotted words:

division   division   division   division   division

What does it mean? Trace the dotted words:

separation; an act of separating a whole into parts.

separation; an act of separating a whole into parts.

Use the word in a sentence. Trace the dotted words:

A sense of division between boys and girls in the class was growing.

A sense of division between boys and girls in the class was growing.

Handwriting Essential, trace the dotted letters:

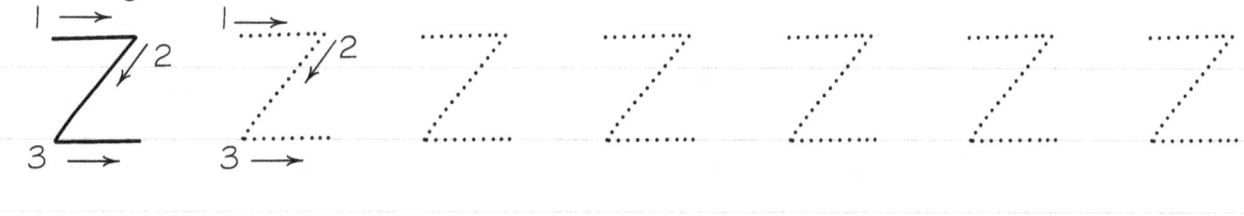

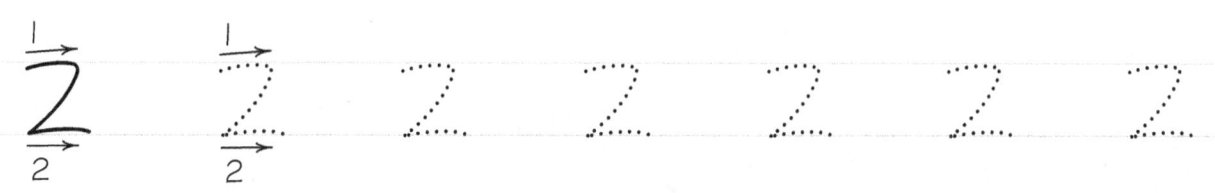

effect | ef-fect | a change caused by an action.

The football hit Tommy and he was stunned. You could see a surprising **effect** on his face.

Trace the dotted words:

effect   effect   effect   effect   effect   effect

What does it mean? Trace the dotted words:

a change caused by an action.
a change caused by an action.

Use the word in a sentence. Trace the dotted words:

The football hit Tommy and he was stunned. You could see a surprising effect on his face.
The football hit Tommy and he was stunned. You could see a surprising effect on his face.

Handwriting Essential, trace the dotted letters:

# # # # # #

36

elect | e-lect | to select by voting.

Let's vote to **elect** a cheerleader.

Trace the dotted words:

elect elect elect elect elect elect elect

What does it mean? Trace the dotted words:

to select by voting.
to select by voting.

Use the word in a sentence. Trace the dotted words:

Let's vote to elect a cheerleader.
Let's vote to elect a cheerleader.

Handwriting Essential, trace the dotted letters:

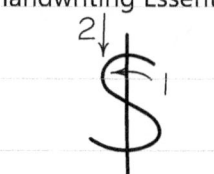 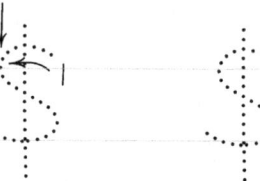 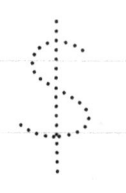 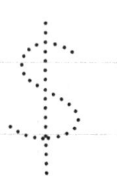 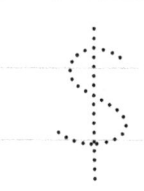

endangered | en-dan-ger-ed | in a state of unsafe; at risk of dying out.

Pandas are one of the **endangered** species.

Trace the dotted words:

endangered   endangered   endangered

What does it mean? Trace the dotted words:

in a state of unsafe; at risk of dying out.
in a state of unsafe; at risk of dying out.

Use the word in a sentence. Trace the dotted words:

Pandas are one of the endangered species.
Pandas are one of the endangered species.

Handwriting Essential, trace the dotted letters:

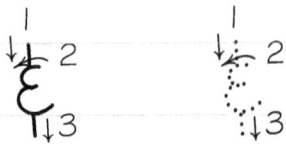

event | e-vent | a thing that occurs.

The coming 4th of July Parade will be a very fun **event**.

Trace the dotted words:

event event event event event event

What does it mean? Trace the dotted words:

a thing that occurs.
a thing that occurs.

Use the word in a sentence. Trace the dotted words:

The coming 4th of July Parade will be a very fun event.
The coming 4th of July Parade will be a very fun event.

Handwriting Essential, trace the dotted letters:

( ) ( ) ( ) ( ) ( ) ( )

examine | ex-am-ine | to inspect or test the condition of.

Cathy leaned down to **examine** a tiny bug on grass.

Trace the dotted words:

examine   examine   examine   examine   examine

What does it mean? Trace the dotted words:

to inspect or test the condition of.
to inspect or test the condition of.

Use the word in a sentence. Trace the dotted words:

Cathy leaned down to examine a tiny bug on grass.
Cathy leaned down to examine a tiny bug on grass.

Handwriting Essential, trace the dotted letters:

example | ex-am-ple | a typical thing of a group that to be imitated or not to be imitated.

Be a good **example**, would you?

Trace the dotted words:

example example example example example

What does it mean? Trace the dotted words:

a typical thing of a group that to be imitated or not to be imitated.
a typical thing of a group that to be imitated or not to be imitated.

Use the word in a sentence. Trace the dotted words:

Be a good example, would you?
Be a good example, would you?

Handwriting Essential, trace the dotted letters:

2 2 2 2 2 2
3 3 3 3 3 3

experience | ex-pe-ri-ence | knowledge and skill from doing and seeing.

It was such an amazing **experience** watching Avatar in a 3D theater. Do you know what 3D is?

Trace the dotted words:

experience   experience   experience   experience

What does it mean? Trace the dotted words:

knowledge and skill from doing and seeing.
knowledge and skill from doing and seeing.

Use the word in a sentence. Trace the dotted words:

It was such an amazing experience watching Avatar in a 3D theater. Do you know what 3D is?
It was such an amazing experience watching Avatar in a 3D theater. Do you know what 3D is?

Handwriting Essential, trace the dotted letters:

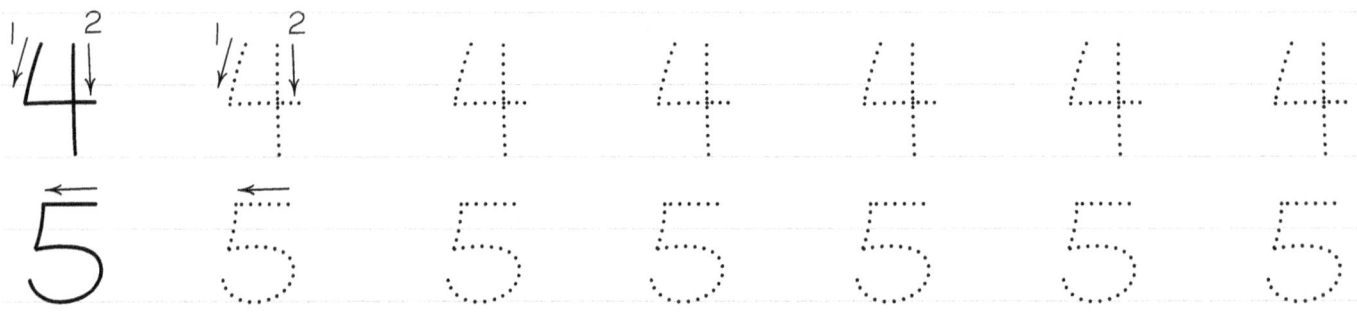

explore | ex-plore | travel to discover; study to find.

I'd love to **explore** the woods. There may be mysterious treasures hidden in there.

Trace the dotted words:

explore   explore   explore   explore   explore

What does it mean? Trace the dotted words:

travel to discover; study to find.
travel to discover; study to find.

Use the word in a sentence. Trace the dotted words:

I'd love to explore the woods. There may be mysterious treasures hidden in there.
I'd love to explore the woods. There may be mysterious treasures hidden in there.

Handwriting Essential, trace the dotted letters:

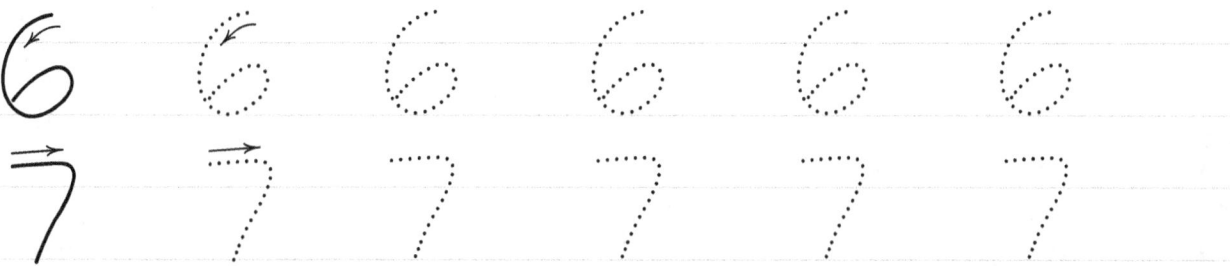

43

fatal | fa-tal | causing death.

War is a **fatal** event. People get killed, children lose their parents, and everything will be destroyed.

Trace the dotted words:

fatal fatal fatal fatal fatal fatal fatal

What does it mean? Trace the dotted words:

causing death.
causing death.

Use the word in a sentence. Trace the dotted words:

War is a fatal event. People get killed, children lose their parents, and everything will be destroyed.
War is a fatal event. People get killed, children lose their parents, and everything will be destroyed.

Handwriting Essential, trace the dotted letters:

8 8 8 8 8 8 8
9 9 9 9 9 9 9

fierce | fierce | showing intense, violent, and forceful.

Where the line between good and bad of playing video games lies is a matter of **fierce** dispute.

Trace the dotted words:

fierce   fierce   fierce   fierce   fierce   fierce

What does it mean? Trace the dotted words:

showing intense, violent, and forceful.
showing intense, violent, and forceful.

Use the word in a sentence. Trace the dotted words:

Where the line between good and bad of playing video games lies is a matter of fierce dispute.
Where the line between good and bad of playing video games lies is a matter of fierce dispute.

Handwriting Essential, trace the dotted letters:

? ? ? ? ? ? ?

flexible | flex-i-ble | able to bend or change easily without breaking.

Can we be more **flexible** about dinner time? I have too much homework to do today.

Trace the dotted words:

flexible   flexible   flexible   flexible   flexible

What does it mean? Trace the dotted words:

able to bend or change easily without breaking.
able to bend or change easily without breaking.

Use the word in a sentence. Trace the dotted words:

Can we be more flexible about dinner time?
I have too much homework to do today.
Can we be more flexible about dinner time?
I have too much homework to do today.

Handwriting Essential, trace the dotted letters:

A B C D E F G H I
J K L M N O P Q
R S T U V W X Y
Z # $ ¢

flutter | flut-ter | a quick and irregular movement.

Jackie waited for a long time. Seeing mom's car finally appeared in front of the entrance, she felt her heart started to **flutter**.

Trace the dotted words:

flutter   flutter   flutter   flutter   flutter   flutter

What does it mean? Trace the dotted words:

a quick and irregular movement.
a quick and irregular movement.

Use the word in a sentence. Trace the dotted words:

Jackie waited for a long time. Seeing mom's car finally appeared in front of the entrance, she felt her heart started to flutter.
Jackie waited for a long time. Seeing mom's car finally appeared in front of the entrance, she felt her heart started to flutter.

fortunate | for-tu-nate | receiving or bringing an unexpected good thing.

I was very **fortunate** to grow up in a time when my parents were still in love with each other. Most of my classmates didn't meet their real father or mother often.

Trace the dotted words:

fortunate   fortunate   fortunate   fortunate

What does it mean? Trace the dotted words:

receiving or bringing an unexpected good thing.
receiving or bringing an unexpected good thing.

Use the word in a sentence. Trace the dotted words:

I was very fortunate to grow up in a time when my parents were still in love with each other. Most of my classmates didn't meet their real father or mother often.
I was very fortunate to grow up in a time when my parents were still in love with each other. Most of my classmates didn't meet their real father or mother often.

frail | frail | unhealthy, weak, or easily broken.

Wearing a big coat, I gave them an impression of me as being **frail** and petite. But I was quite beefy and strong. I was a gymnast in school and I had lots of muscles.

Trace the dotted words:

frail frail frail frail frail frail frail frail

What does it mean? Trace the dotted words:

unhealthy, weak, or easily broken.
unhealthy, weak, or easily broken.

Use the word in a sentence. Trace the dotted words:

Wearing a big coat, I gave them an impression of me as being frail and petite. But I was quite beefy and strong. I was a gymnast in school and I had lots of muscles.

Wearing a big coat, I gave them an impression of me as being frail and petite. But I was quite beefy and strong. I was a gymnast in school and I had lots of muscles.

furious | fu-ri-ous | very angry, violent, and forceful.

Mrs. Balloons would have been **furious** if we hadn't cleaned up that mess quickly.

Trace the dotted words:

furious   furious   furious   furious   furious

What does it mean? Trace the dotted words:

very angry, violent, and forceful.
very angry, violent, and forceful.

Use the word in a sentence. Trace the dotted words:

Mrs. Balloons would have been furious if we hadn't cleaned up that mess quickly.
Mrs. Balloons would have been furious if we hadn't cleaned up that mess quickly.

Handwriting Essential, trace the dotted letters:

a b c d e f g h i j k l
m n o p q r s t u v w
x y z
1 2 3 4 5 6 7 8 9 0

gathered | gath-er-ed | coming or bringing together from different places.

My friends **gathered** at my house. We sat around, talked, ate, and laughed. It was fun.

Trace the dotted words:

gathered   gathered   gathered   gathered

What does it mean? Trace the dotted words:

coming or bringing together from different places.
coming or bringing together from different places.

Use the word in a sentence. Trace the dotted words:

My friends gathered at my house. We sat around, talked, ate, and laughed. It was fun.
My friends gathered at my house. We sat around, talked, ate, and laughed. It was fun.

Handwriting Essential, trace the dotted letters:

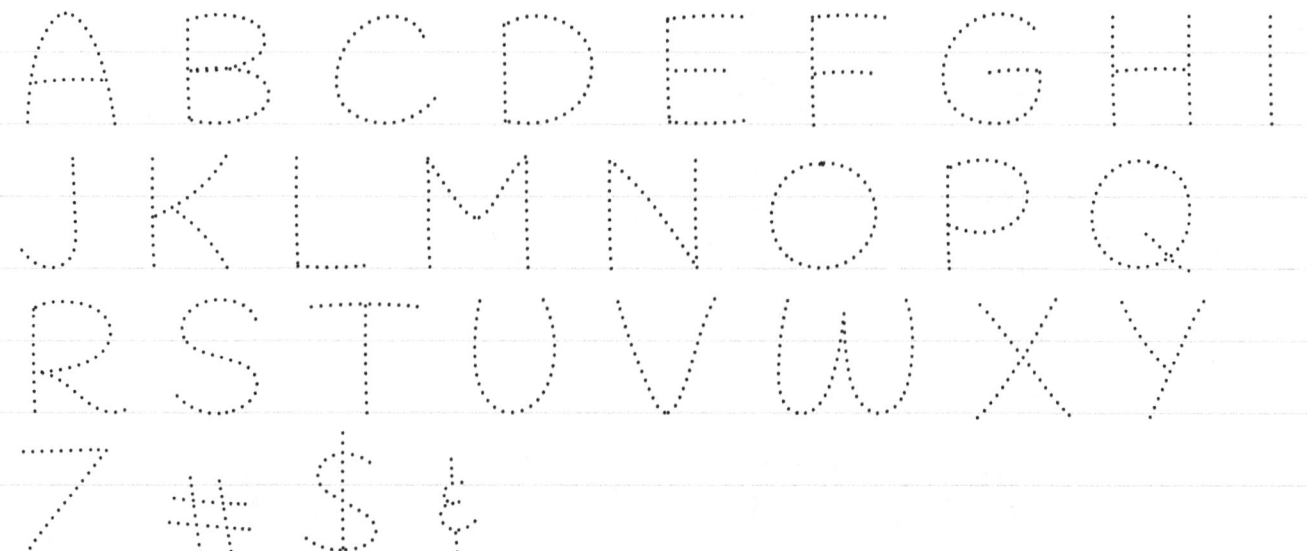

gist | gist | the main point of information.

Please try to think of a short phrase that sums up the **gist** of the story.

Trace the dotted words:

gist   gist   gist   gist   gist   gist   gist   gist

What does it mean? Trace the dotted words:

the main point of information.
the main point of information.

Use the word in a sentence. Trace the dotted words:

Please try to think of a short phrase that sums up the gist of the story.
Please try to think of a short phrase that sums up the gist of the story.

Handwriting Essential, trace the dotted letters:

a b c d e f g h i j k l
m n o p q r s t u v w
x y z
1 2 3 4 5 6 7 8 9 0

globe | globe | rounded object; the world.

Humans are amazing creatures. We produce 4 babies on this **globe** every second, 360,000 a day. Poor earth!

Trace the dotted words:

globe globe globe globe globe globe

What does it mean? Trace the dotted words:

rounded object; the world.
rounded object; the world.

Use the word in a sentence. Trace the dotted words:

Humans are amazing creatures. We produce 4 babies on this globe every second, 360,000 a day. Poor earth!
Humans are amazing creatures. We produce 4 babies on this globe every second, 360,000 a day. Poor earth!

gradual | grad-u-al | developing slowly in small steps.

Everything in the world is conducted by a **gradual** process. This seems to be the great principle of harmony in the universe.

Trace the dotted words:

gradual   gradual   gradual   gradual   gradual

What does it mean? Trace the dotted words:

developing slowly in small steps.
developing slowly in small steps.

Use the word in a sentence. Trace the dotted words:

Everything in the world is conducted by a gradual process. This seems to be the great principle of harmony in the universe.
Everything in the world is conducted by a gradual process. This seems to be the great principle of harmony in the universe.

individual

| individual | a single person or thing.

If every **individual** has the right amount of food and exercise, not too little and not too much, that's the safest way to health.

Trace the dotted words:

individual   individual   individual   individual

What does it mean? Trace the dotted words:

a single person or thing.
a single person or thing.

Use the word in a sentence. Trace the dotted words:

If every individual has the right amount of food and exercise, not too little and not too much, that's the safest way to health.
If every individual has the right amount of food and exercise, not too little and not too much, that's the safest way to health.

infer | in-fer | to draw a conclusion from facts.

I don't mind my friends, teachers, mom, and daddy to **infer** that
I have all kinds of clever ideas in my not-so-little brain.

Trace the dotted words:

infer   infer   infer   infer   infer   infer   infer

What does it mean? Trace the dotted words:

to draw a conclusion from facts.
to draw a conclusion from facts.

Use the word in a sentence. Trace the dotted words:

I don't mind my friends, teachers, mom, and daddy to infer that I have all kinds of clever ideas in my not-so-little brain.
I don't mind my friends, teachers, mom, and daddy to infer that I have all kinds of clever ideas in my not-so-little brain.

intelligent | in-tel-li-gent | having the ability to learn and understand.

To be **intelligent**, one will need to be flexible and go with the flow, not to be stubborn and self-centered.

Trace the dotted words:

intelligent   intelligent   intelligent

What does it mean? Trace the dotted words:

having the ability to learn and understand.
having the ability to learn and understand.

Use the word in a sentence. Trace the dotted words:

To be intelligent, one will need to be flexible and go with the flow, not to be stubborn and self-centered.
To be intelligent, one will need to be flexible and go with the flow, not to be stubborn and self-centered.

invitation | in-vi-ta-tion | the act of inviting someone to do something.

Making a good smile is an expression of warm **invitation**;
it is an invitation to happiness in our common humanity.

Trace the dotted words:

invitation   invitation   invitation   invitation

What does it mean? Trace the dotted words:

the act of inviting someone to do something.
the act of inviting someone to do something.

Use the word in a sentence. Trace the dotted words:

Making a good smile is an expression of warm invitation; it is an invitation to happiness in our common humanity.
Making a good smile is an expression of warm invitation; it is an invitation to happiness in our common humanity.

irritate | ir-ri-tate | to make someone annoyed.

Bobby scratched his head, **irritated** at himself for getting so caught up in the fact that Fred didn't want to play with him.

Trace the dotted words:

irritate irritate irritate irritate irritate

What does it mean? Trace the dotted words:

to make someone annoyed.
to make someone annoyed.

Use the word in a sentence. Trace the dotted words:

Bobby scratched his head, irritated at himself for getting so caught up in the fact that Fred didn't want to play with him.
Bobby scratched his head, irritated at himself for getting so caught up in the fact that Fred didn't want to play with him.

journey | jour-ney | an act of traveling; travel.

"We know it's a long **journey** from Canada to Disney World at Florida. But be ready, we're coming!"

Trace the dotted words:

journey journey journey journey journey

What does it mean? Trace the dotted words:

an act of traveling; travel.
an act of traveling; travel.

Use the word in a sentence. Trace the dotted words:

"We know it's a long journey from Canada to Disney World at Florida. But be ready, we're coming!"
"We know it's a long journey from Canada to Disney World at Florida. But be ready, we're coming!"

limit | lim-it | the amount, level, or number beyond the point that may pass.

There's no **limit** to how smart a child can get, on account of one creative saying always leading to another.

Trace the dotted words:

limit   limit   limit   limit   limit   limit   limit

What does it mean? Trace the dotted words:

the amount, level, or number beyond the point that may pass.

the amount, level, or number beyond the point that may pass.

Use the word in a sentence. Trace the dotted words:

There's no limit to how smart a child can get, on account of one creative saying always leading to another.

There's no limit to how smart a child can get, on account of one creative saying always leading to another.

magnificent | mag-nif-i-cent | very good, great, or admirable.

"You're one of the most **magnificent** and delightful presents God has given us."

Trace the dotted words:

magnificent magnificent magnificent magnificent

What does it mean? Trace the dotted words:

very good, great, or admirable.
very good, great, or admirable.

Use the word in a sentence. Trace the dotted words:

"You're one of the most magnificent and delightful presents God has given us."
"You're one of the most magnificent and delightful presents God has given us."

mend | mend | to fix something that is broken.

I have to **mend** my relation with Amy quickly because she will bring cupcakes for her birthday tomorrow. I really like cupcakes.

Trace the dotted words:

mend   mend   mend   mend   mend   mend   mend

What does it mean? Trace the dotted words:

to fix something that is broken.
to fix something that is broken.

Use the word in a sentence. Trace the dotted words:

I have to mend my relation with Amy quickly because she will bring cupcakes for her birthday tomorrow. I really like cupcakes.
I have to mend my relation with Amy quickly because she will bring cupcakes for her birthday tomorrow. I really like cupcakes.

multiply | mul-ti-ply | to increase itself for a number of times.

To make the "multiply" really meaningful, I hope my chocolate candy bars can multiply ten times, like 2x10=20.

Trace the dotted words:

multiply   multiply   multiply   multiply   multiply

What does it mean? Trace the dotted words:

to increase itself for a number of times.
to increase itself for a number of times.

Use the word in a sentence. Trace the dotted words:

To make the "multiply" really meaningful, I hope my chocolate candy bars can multiply ten times, like 2x10=20.
To make the "multiply" really meaningful, I hope my chocolate candy bars can multiply ten times, like 2x10=20.

mystify | mys-ti-fy | to purposely make something unintelligible.

I don't know why my brain is so smart. I am always surprised and **mystified** by it.

Trace the dotted words:

mystify   mystify   mystify   mystify   mystify

What does it mean? Trace the dotted words:

to purposely make something unintelligible.
to purposely make something unintelligible.

Use the word in a sentence. Trace the dotted words:

I don't know why my brain is so smart. I am always surprised and mystified by it.
I don't know why my brain is so smart. I am always surprised and mystified by it.

nation | na-tion | a country with its own government.

I pledge allegiance to my Flag and the Republic for which it stands, one **nation**, indivisible, with liberty and justice for all.

Trace the dotted words:

nation   nation   nation   nation   nation   nation

What does it mean? Trace the dotted words:

a country with its own government.
a country with its own government.

Use the word in a sentence. Trace the dotted words:

I pledge allegiance to my Flag and the Republic for which it stands, one nation, indivisible, with liberty and justice for all.
I pledge allegiance to my Flag and the Republic for which it stands, one nation, indivisible, with liberty and justice for all.

nervous | nerv-ous | anxious and worried.

I always got **nervous** speaking in front of the class. The first sentence, I was **nervous**. Then after that, forget it; I'd start talking.

Trace the dotted words:

nervous   nervous   nervous   nervous   nervous

What does it mean? Trace the dotted words:

anxious and worried.
anxious and worried.

Use the word in a sentence. Trace the dotted words:

I always got nervous speaking in front of the class. The first sentence, I was nervous. Then after that, forget it; I'd start talking.
I always got nervous speaking in front of the class. The first sentence, I was nervous. Then after that, forget it; I'd start talking.

observe | ob-serve | to notice or to watch carefully.

I listen and talk; I also watch and **observe**. That's communication.

Trace the dotted words:

observe   observe   observe   observe   observe

What does it mean? Trace the dotted words:

to notice or to watch carefully.
to notice or to watch carefully.

Use the word in a sentence. Trace the dotted words:

I listen and talk; I also watch and observe. That's communication.
I listen and talk; I also watch and observe. That's communication.

occur | nerv-ous | to happen or take place.

That was an accident that **occured** right after lunch. I crashed into Miss Honey and knocked her down to the floor.

Trace the dotted words:

occur   occur   occur   occur   occur   occur

What does it mean? Trace the dotted words:

to happen or take place.
to happen or take place.

Use the word in a sentence. Trace the dotted words:

That was an accident that occured right after lunch. I crashed into Miss Honey and knocked her down to the floor.
That was an accident that occured right after lunch. I crashed into Miss Honey and knocked her down to the floor.

opponent | op-po-nent | a person who competes against another.

It's not about knocking my **opponent** out.

It's about I don't fail.

Trace the dotted words:

opponent   opponent   opponent   opponent

What does it mean? Trace the dotted words:

a person who competes against another.
a person who competes against another.

Use the word in a sentence. Trace the dotted words:

It's not about knocking my opponent out.
It's about I don't fail.
It's not about knocking my opponent out.
It's about I don't fail.

opposite | op-po-site | a position on the other side of something; totally different.

Cathy made a face as she sat in the chair **opposite** her mom, "Okay, let's talk."

Trace the dotted words:

opposite   opposite   opposite   opposite

What does it mean? Trace the dotted words:

a position on the other side of something; totally different.
a position on the other side of something; totally different.

Use the word in a sentence. Trace the dotted words:

Cathy made a face as she sat in the chair opposite her mom, "Okay, let's talk."
Cathy made a face as she sat in the chair opposite her mom, "Okay, let's talk."

ordeal | or-deal | a long lasting unpleasant experience.

We're grateful for the fifteen minutes recess after a boring History class.
But we also realize the **ordeal** that lies before us, a long Math class.

Trace the dotted words:

ordeal   ordeal   ordeal   ordeal   ordeal   ordeal

What does it mean? Trace the dotted words:

a long lasting unpleasant experience.
a long lasting unpleasant experience.

Use the word in a sentence. Trace the dotted words:

We're grateful for the fifteen minutes recess after a boring History class. But we also realize the ordeal that lies before us, a long Math class.
We're grateful for the fifteen minutes recess after a boring History class. But we also realize the ordeal that lies before us, a long Math class.

origin | or-i-gin | the beginning; the cause.

The DNA test can trace my ancestral **origin** back 1,000 years.

I hope my ancestor was not a monkey, you know, 1,000 years!

Trace the dotted words:

origin   origin   origin   origin   origin   origin

What does it mean? Trace the dotted words:

the beginning; the cause.
the beginning; the cause.

Use the word in a sentence. Trace the dotted words:

The DNA test can trace my ancestral origin back 1,000 years. I hope my ancestor was not a monkey, you know, 1,000 years!
The DNA test can trace my ancestral origin back 1,000 years. I hope my ancestor was not a monkey, you know, 1,000 years!

outcome | out-come | result or effect.

If aliens visit us, I hope the **outcome** won't be like when Columbus landed in America. Bad idea for the native earth mankind.

Trace the dotted words:

outcome   outcome   outcome   outcome   outcome

What does it mean? Trace the dotted words:

result or effect.
result or effect.

Use the word in a sentence. Trace the dotted words:

If aliens visit us, I hope the outcome won't be like when Columbus landed in America. Bad idea for the native earth mankind.
If aliens visit us, I hope the outcome won't be like when Columbus landed in America. Bad idea for the native earth mankind.

passage | pas-sage | a gate or way that connects places.

I squeezed through a narrow **passage** on the wall and stepped into an aisle leading to an exit. I escaped safely though a little out of breath.

Trace the dotted words:

passage   passage   passage   passage   passage

What does it mean? Trace the dotted words:

a gate or way that connects places.
a gate or way that connects places.

Use the word in a sentence. Trace the dotted words:

I squeezed through a narrow passage on the wall and stepped into an aisle leading to an exit. I escaped safely though a little out of breath.
I squeezed through a narrow passage on the wall and stepped into an aisle leading to an exit. I escaped safely though a little out of breath.

patient | pa-tient | able to tolerate annoyed things; one who receives medical care.

We all need to be **patient** and give each other a little space.

Trace the dotted words:

patient   patient   patient   patient   patient   patient

What does it mean? Trace the dotted words:

able to tolerate annoyed things; one who receives medical care.
able to tolerate annoyed things; one who receives medical care.

Use the word in a sentence. Trace the dotted words:

We all need to be patient and give each other a little space.
We all need to be patient and give each other a little space.

peer | peer | to look carefully; someone who has the same social position.

The microscope allows us to **peer** deeper into the mysteries of cells in your body.

Trace the dotted words:

peer   peer   peer   peer   peer   peer   peer

What does it mean? Trace the dotted words:

to look carefully; someone who has the same social position.
to look carefully; someone who has the same social position.

Use the word in a sentence. Trace the dotted words:

The microscope allows us to peer deeper into the mysteries of cells in your body.
The microscope allows us to peer deeper into the mysteries of cells in your body.

persuade | per-suade | to make someone believe something.

How did you **persuade** daddy to agree to buy you a new robotic servant?

Trace the dotted words:

persuade   persuade   persuade   persuade

What does it mean? Trace the dotted words:

to make someone believe something.
to make someone believe something.

Use the word in a sentence. Trace the dotted words:

How did you persuade daddy to agree to buy you a new robotic servant?
How did you persuade daddy to agree to buy you a new robotic servant?

pleasant | pleas-ant | a sense of happiness and enjoyment.

There are more **pleasant** things to do than argue with an idiot.

Trace the dotted words:

pleasant   pleasant   pleasant   pleasant

What does it mean? Trace the dotted words:

a sense of happiness and enjoyment.
a sense of happiness and enjoyment.

Use the word in a sentence. Trace the dotted words:

There are more pleasant things to do than argue with an idiot.
There are more pleasant things to do than argue with an idiot.

predict | pre-dict | to say something that will happen in the future.

Everything changes with time. You can't predict it all.

You can't even **predict** what's in your dream tonight.

Trace the dotted words:

predict   predict   predict   predict   predict

What does it mean? Trace the dotted words:

to say something that will happen in the future.
to say something that will happen in the future.

Use the word in a sentence. Trace the dotted words:

Everything changes with time. You can't predict it all. You can't even predict what's in your dream tonight.
Everything changes with time. You can't predict it all. You can't even predict what's in your dream tonight.

prevent | pre-vent | to keep something from existing or occurring.

This vaccine will **prevent** us from getting sick.

Trace the dotted words:

prevent   prevent   prevent   prevent   prevent

What does it mean? Trace the dotted words:

to keep something from existing or occurring.
to keep something from existing or occurring.

Use the word in a sentence. Trace the dotted words:

This vaccine will prevent us from getting sick.
This vaccine will prevent us from getting sick.

primary | pri-ma-ry | original; the most important part.

The primary goal of space science is to discover what's unknown about the space. Actually, any science is about to discover things unknown.

Trace the dotted words:

primary   primary   primary   primary   primary

What does it mean? Trace the dotted words:

original; the most important part.
original; the most important part.

Use the word in a sentence. Trace the dotted words:

The primary goal of space science is to discover what's unknown about the space. Actually, any science is about to discover things unknown.
The primary goal of space science is to discover what's unknown about the space. Actually, any science is about to discover things unknown.

purpose | pur-pose | the reason to do something; the reason something exists.

What is the purpose of you saying that? Just try to make me feel bad?

Trace the dotted words:

purpose   purpose   purpose   purpose   purpose

What does it mean? Trace the dotted words:

the reason to do something; the reason something exists.
the reason to do something; the reason something exists.

Use the word in a sentence. Trace the dotted words:

What is the purpose of you saying that? Just try to make me feel bad?
What is the purpose of you saying that? Just try to make me feel bad?

recognize | rec-og-nize | to acknowledge someone or something you knew.

I couldn't **recognize** myself in the mirror at first with the new makeup. It's so cool.

Trace the dotted words:

recognize   recognize   recognize   recognize

What does it mean? Trace the dotted words:

to acknowledge someone or something you knew.
to acknowledge someone or something you knew.

Use the word in a sentence. Trace the dotted words:

I couldn't recognize myself in the mirror at first with the new makeup. It's so cool.
I couldn't recognize myself in the mirror at first with the new makeup. It's so cool.

repair | re-pair | to fix something that is broken.

The greatness of America lies not in being more enlightened than any other nation, but rather in her ability to **repair** her faults.

Trace the dotted words:

repair   repair   repair   repair   repair   repair

What does it mean? Trace the dotted words:

to fix something that is broken.
to fix something that is broken.

Use the word in a sentence. Trace the dotted words:

The greatness of America lies not in being more enlightened than any other nation, but rather in her ability to repair her faults.
The greatness of America lies not in being more enlightened than any other nation, but rather in her ability to repair her faults.

respect | re-spect | an admiring feeling for someone or something.

With all due **respect**, Miss Honey, I don't think you're right in this case.

Trace the dotted words:

respect   respect   respect   respect   respect

What does it mean? Trace the dotted words:

an admiring feeling for someone or something.
an admiring feeling for someone or something.

Use the word in a sentence. Trace the dotted words:

With all due respect, Miss Honey, I don't think you're right in this case.
With all due respect, Miss Honey, I don't think you're right in this case.

responsible | re-spon-si-ble | obligated to; having control over or duty to care.

My mom is **responsible** for cooking Christmas dinner and my dad is in charge of decorating our house.

Trace the dotted words:

responsible   responsible   responsible

What does it mean? Trace the dotted words:

obligated to; having control over or duty to care.
obligated to; having control over or duty to care.

Use the word in a sentence. Trace the dotted words:

My mom is responsible for cooking Christmas dinner and my dad is in charge of decorating our house.
My mom is responsible for cooking Christmas dinner and my dad is in charge of decorating our house.

ridiculous | re-spect | unreasonable, silly, and stupid.

I have never made but one prayer to God, a very short one:
'O Lord make my enemies ridiculous.' And God granted it.

Trace the dotted words:

ridiculous   ridiculous   ridiculous   ridiculous

What does it mean? Trace the dotted words:

unreasonable, silly, and stupid.
unreasonable, silly, and stupid

Use the word in a sentence. Trace the dotted words:

I have never made but one prayer to God, a very short one: 'O Lord make my enemies ridiculous.' And God granted it.
I have never made but one prayer to God, a very short one: 'O Lord make my enemies ridiculous.' And God granted it

scatter | scat-ter | to move randomly far apart.

The zebras quickly scattered as the lion charged at the herd.

Trace the dotted words:

scatter   scatter   scatter   scatter   scatter

What does it mean? Trace the dotted words:

to move randomly far apart.
to move randomly far apart.

Use the word in a sentence. Trace the dotted words:

The zebras quickly scattered as the lion charged at the herd.
The zebras quickly scattered as the lion charged at the herd.

sensitive | sen-si-tive | highly responsive to minor changes.

This metal detector is so cool. It's **sensitive** enough to detect coins buried 2 feet underground.

Trace the dotted words:

sensitive   sensitive   sensitive   sensitive   sensitive

What does it mean? Trace the dotted words:

highly responsive to minor changes.
highly responsive to minor changes.

Use the word in a sentence. Trace the dotted words:

This metal detector is so cool. It's sensitive enough to detect coins buried 2 feet underground.
This metal detector is so cool. It's sensitive enough to detect coins buried 2 feet underground.

shiver | shiv-er | shaking slightly because of cold or frightened.

"It's so cold," she said with a **shiver**.

Trace the dotted words:

shiver   shiver   shiver   shiver   shiver   shiver

What does it mean? Trace the dotted words:

shaking slightly because of cold or frightened.
shaking slightly because of cold or frightened.

Use the word in a sentence. Trace the dotted words:

"It's so cold," she said with a shiver.
"It's so cold," she said with a shiver.

signal | sig-nal | a gesture, action, or sound that conveys message.

The phone **signal** was not strong enough for me to make a phone call to my friends.

Trace the dotted words:

signal signal signal signal signal signal

What does it mean? Trace the dotted words:

a gesture, action, or sound that conveys message.
a gesture, action, or sound that conveys message.

Use the word in a sentence. Trace the dotted words:

The phone signal was not strong enough for me to make a phone call to my friends.
The phone signal was not strong enough for me to make a phone call to my friends.

similar | sim-i-lar | alike but not exactly the same.

Your phone is **similar** to mine in shape and color.

Trace the dotted words:

similar   similar   similar   similar   similar

What does it mean? Trace the dotted words:

alike but not exactly the same.
alike but not exactly the same.

Use the word in a sentence. Trace the dotted words:

Your phone is similar to mine in shape and color.
Your phone is similar to mine in shape and color.

slumber | slum-ber | in the state of sleep; to sleep.

What's a **slumber** party? It's a sleepover. That's it.

Trace the dotted words:

slumber   slumber   slumber   slumber   slumber

What does it mean? Trace the dotted words:

in the state of sleep; to sleep.
in the state of sleep; to sleep.

Use the word in a sentence. Trace the dotted words:

What's a slumber party? It's a sleepover. That's it.
What's a slumber party? It's a sleepover. That's it.

solution | so-lu-tion | an answer to a problem or difficult situation.

I have a **solution** that might save the world. Let's all move to Mars.

Trace the dotted words:

solution   solution   solution   solution   solution

What does it mean? Trace the dotted words:

an answer to a problem or difficult situation.
an answer to a problem or difficult situation.

Use the word in a sentence. Trace the dotted words:

I have a solution that might save the world. Let's all move to Mars.
I have a solution that might save the world. Let's all move to Mars.

starve | starve | hungry; to feel severe hunger.

I grew up wanting to be an artist, but my parents were sure I would **starve** to death. So, they put me in a kitchen to become a chef.

Trace the dotted words:

starve   starve   starve   starve   starve   starve

What does it mean? Trace the dotted words:

hungry; to feel severe hunger.
hungry; to feel severe hunger.

Use the word in a sentence. Trace the dotted words:

I grew up wanting to be an artist, but my parents were sure I would starve to death. So, they put me in a kitchen to become a chef.
I grew up wanting to be an artist, but my parents were sure I would starve to death. So, they put me in a kitchen to become a chef.

struggled | strug-gled | feeling great difficult and resistant.

I **struggled** to be good at math, to be good at writing, to be good at whatever... But what I did not struggle with is the best of what I do, like telling stories.

Trace the dotted words:

struggled   struggled   struggled   struggled

What does it mean? Trace the dotted words:

feeling great difficult and resistant.
feeling great difficult and resistant.

Use the word in a sentence. Trace the dotted words:

I struggled to be good at math, to be good at writing, to be good at whatever... But what I did not struggle with is the best of what I do, like telling stories.
I struggled to be good at math, to be good at writing, to be good at whatever... But what I did not struggle with is the best of what I do, like telling stories.

stumble | stum-ble | to fall or lose balance while walking or running.

Alex was running in the woods. He **stumbled** on a log, fell into the thick bushes, and hurt his butt.

Trace the dotted words:

stumble   stumble   stumble   stumble   stumble

What does it mean? Trace the dotted words:

to fall or lose balance while walking or running.
to fall or lose balance while walking or running.

Use the word in a sentence. Trace the dotted words:

Alex was running in the woods. He stumbled on a log, fell into the thick bushes, and hurt his butt.
Alex was running in the woods. He stumbled on a log, fell into the thick bushes, and hurt his butt.

tackle | tack-le | to deal with a problem or difficult situation.

A bowl of ice cream always calms me down and makes my thoughts straight. Then I can **tackle** the problem with a fresh mind. But it does get me fat though.

Trace the dotted words:

tackle   tackle   tackle   tackle   tackle   tackle

What does it mean? Trace the dotted words:

to deal with a problem or difficult situation.
to deal with a problem or difficult situation.

Use the word in a sentence. Trace the dotted words:

A bowl of ice cream always calms me down and makes my thoughts straight. Then I can tackle the problem with a fresh mind. But it does get me fat though.
A bowl of ice cream always calms me down and makes my thoughts straight. Then I can tackle the problem with a fresh mind. But it does get me fat though.

triumph | tri-umph | a big victory, success, or achievement, or the feeling of it.

One of the greatest **triumphs** of human history is the eradication of smallpox by vaccination.

Trace the dotted words:

triumph   triumph   triumph   triumph   triumph

What does it mean? Trace the dotted words:

a big victory, success, or achievement, or the feeling of it.
a big victory, success, or achievement, or the feeling of it.

Use the word in a sentence. Trace the dotted words:

One of the greatest triumphs of human history is the eradication of smallpox by vaccination.
One of the greatest triumphs of human history is the eradication of smallpox by vaccination.

typical | typ-i-cal | the essential facts or qualities of a group of things or people.

This has been a **typical** day for me, having breakfast, going to school, coming back home, having dinner, doing homework, and going to bed. No time to play.

Trace the dotted words:

typical   typical   typical   typical   typical   typical

What does it mean? Trace the dotted words:

the essential facts or qualities of a group of things or people.

the essential facts or qualities of a group of things or people.

Use the word in a sentence. Trace the dotted words:

This has been a typical day for me, having breakfast, going to school, coming back home, having dinner, doing homework, and going to bed. No time to play.

This has been a typical day for me, having breakfast, going to school, coming back home, having dinner, doing homework, and going to bed. No time to play.

unite | u-nite | to come together for a common goal.

What's the capital of the **United** States? Washington, D.C.

Trace the dotted words:

unite unite unite unite unite unite unite

What does it mean? Trace the dotted words:

to come together for a common goal.
to come together for a common goal.

Use the word in a sentence. Trace the dotted words:

What's the capital of the United States? Washington, D.C.
What's the capital of the United States? Washington, D.C.

unusual | un-u-su-al | different from commonly known.

Humans are a very, very unusual species. We dive deep in the sea, fly high in the sky, and send instant messages around the globe.

Trace the dotted words:

unusual unusual unusual unusual unusual

What does it mean? Trace the dotted words:

different from commonly known.
different from commonly known.

Use the word in a sentence. Trace the dotted words:

Humans are a very, very unusual species. We dive deep in the sea, fly high in the sky, and send instant messages around the globe.
Humans are a very, very unusual species. We dive deep in the sea, fly high in the sky, and send instant messages around the globe.

valuable | val-u-a-ble | very useful, or worth a lot of money.

what's the most **valuable** thing for now? The cupcake in my hands.

Trace the dotted words:

valuable   valuable   valuable   valuable   valuable

What does it mean? Trace the dotted words:

very useful, or worth a lot of money.
very useful, or worth a lot of money.

Use the word in a sentence. Trace the dotted words:

what's the most valuable thing for now? The cupcake in my hands.
what's the most valuable thing for now? The cupcake in my hands.

vast | vast | extremely great in amount, size, or intensity.

The **vast** majority of students in my class agreed that we should celebrate Miss Honey's birthday.

Trace the dotted words:

vast vast vast vast vast vast vast vast

What does it mean? Trace the dotted words:

extremely great in amount, size, or intensity.
extremely great in amount, size, or intensity.

Use the word in a sentence. Trace the dotted words:

The vast majority of students in my class agreed that we should celebrate Miss Honey's birthday.
The vast majority of students in my class agreed that we should celebrate Miss Honey's birthday.

vision | vi-sion | the state of seeing; the mental images of something.

America was established to realize a **vision**, to realize an ideal – to discover and maintain liberty among men.

Trace the dotted words:

valuable   valuable   valuable   valuable   valuable

What does it mean? Trace the dotted words:

the state of seeing; the mental images of something.
the state of seeing; the mental images of something.

Use the word in a sentence. Trace the dotted words:

America was established to realize a vision, to realize an ideal – to discover and maintain liberty among men.
America was established to realize a vision, to realize an ideal – to discover and maintain liberty among men.

volunteer | vol-un-teer | a person who undertakes a task willingly and not getting paid.

"Why do **volunteers** work for free?"

"Because they earn credits that worth more than money."

Trace the dotted words:

vast   vast   vast   vast   vast   vast   vast   vast

What does it mean? Trace the dotted words:

a person who undertakes a task willingly and not getting paid.

a person who undertakes a task willingly and not getting paid.

Use the word in a sentence. Trace the dotted words:

"Why do volunteers work for free?"
"Because they earn credits that worth more than money."
"Why do volunteers work for free?"
"Because they earn credits that worth more than money."

wander | wan-der | to walk leisurely.

"Honey, don't **wander** far from the house. There're strangers on the street."

"Are there any good strangers?"

"Yes. But we're concerning the bad ones."

Trace the dotted words:

wander   wander   wander   wander   wander

What does it mean? Trace the dotted words:

to walk leisurely.
to walk leisurely.

Use the word in a sentence. Trace the dotted words:

"Honey, don't wander far from the house. There're strangers on the street."
"Are there any good strangers?"
"Yes. But we're concerning the bad ones."
"Honey, don't wander far from the house. There're strangers on the street."
"Are there any good strangers?"
"Yes. But we're concerning the bad ones."

Thank you for learning and practicing the 101 academic words with this book. Now you know more than what you usually learn from school. You're better, more intelligent, and smarter. Congratulations!

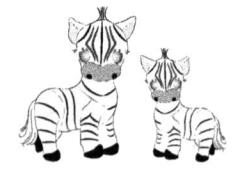

This is a Derek Schuger's work.

www.ingramcontent.com/pod-product-compliance
Lightning Source LLC
Chambersburg PA
CBHW081435220526
45466CB00008B/2402